3 times the charm!

How would you like to sew dozens of colorful fabrics into one quilt top—in a single day? Just think small! And fun! These seven easy little quilts by Me & My Sister Designs use charm packs (pre-cut 5" fabric squares) and a minimum of additional yardage.

Choose your favorite charm pack, or cut a stack of coordinating 5" squares from your fabric stash or scrap bag. Barb and Mary made each design three times to help you visualize your quilt in different colors. The piecing is quick and simple, and the projects are perfect for table toppers, wall hangings, and baby blankies!

me & my sister designs

For Barbara Groves and Mary Jacobson, getting started in the quilt design business began with their very first quilting class.

The quilt shop hosting their beginner's class was for sale, which made the sisters think how much fun it would be to have their own shop. Years later, they did indeed open a quilt shop. Designing and sewing samples for the store was one of their favorite things to do. Eventually, they sold the store to give their full attention to designing quilts—and that was the beginning of Me & My Sister Designs. They've been quilting together for fifteen creative years, and this is their fourth pattern book available through www.LeisureArts.com. To see the sweet and whimsical fabrics that Barb and Mary have designed for Moda, visit MeAndMySisterDesigns.com.

LEISURE ARTS, INC.
Little Rock, Arkansas

amanda

Finished Size: 19³/₄" x 19³/₄" (50 cm x 50 cm)
Finished Block Size: 5" x 5" (13 cm x 13 cm)

fabric requirements

Yardage is based on 43"/44" (109 cm/112 cm) wide fabric.
   1 Charm Pack *or* 28 assorted 5" x 5" squares
   ¹/₄ yd (23 cm) binding fabric
   ⁷/₈ yd (80 cm) backing fabric
You will also need:
   28" x 28" (71 cm x 71 cm) piece of batting

cutting the pieces

*Follow **Rotary Cutting**, page 31, to cut fabric. Cut binding strips from the selvage-to-selvage width of the fabric. All measurements include ¹/₄" seam allowances.*

From Charm Pack or assorted squares:

- Select 9 squares for block centers. From *each* of these, cut 1 **square** 3¹/₂" x 3¹/₂" and 1 **small rectangle** 1¹/₂" x 4¹/₂" (**cutting diagram A**).
- Select 9 squares for remainder of Blocks. From *each* of these, cut 3 **small rectangles** 1¹/₂" x 4¹/₂" (**cutting diagram B**).
- Select 10 squares for borders. From *each* of these, cut 2 **large rectangles** 2¹/₂" x 5" (**cutting diagram C**).

From binding fabric:

- Cut 3 **binding strips** 2¹/₄" wide.

Charm Cutting Diagram A

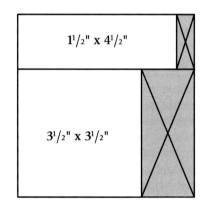

Charm Cutting Diagram B

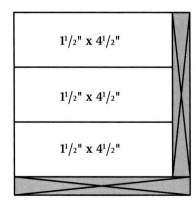

Charm Cutting Diagram C

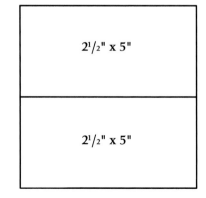

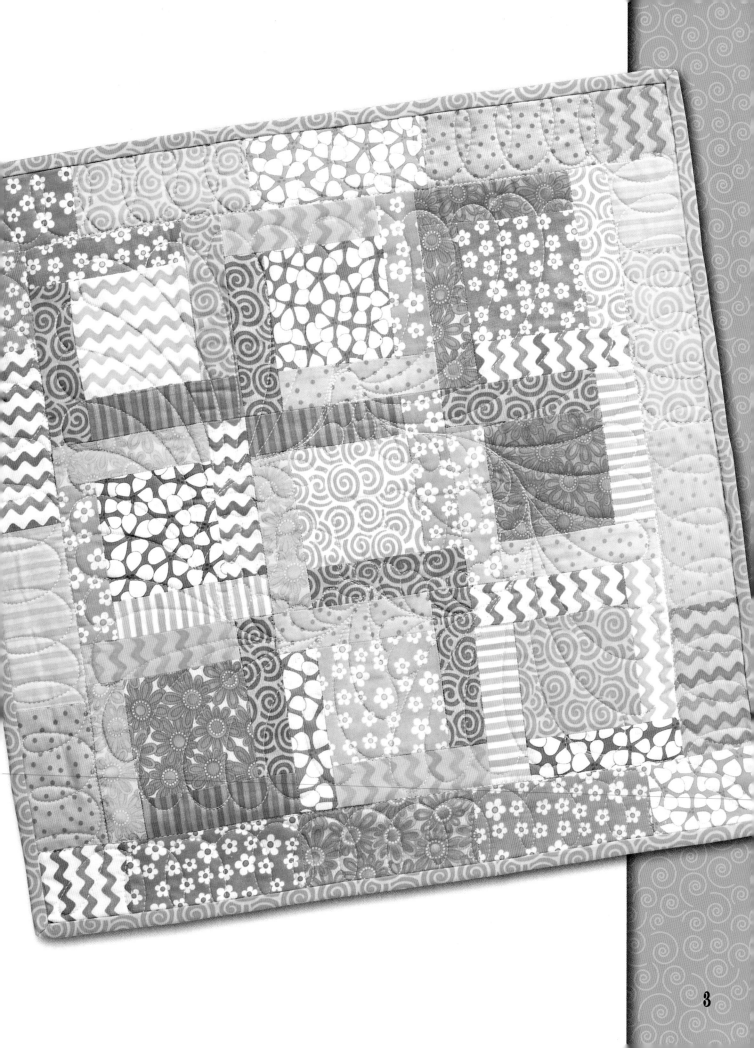

Fig. 1   **Fig. 2**

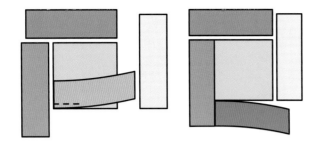

Block (make 9)

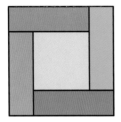

Row (make 3)

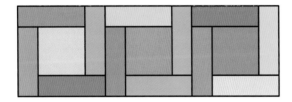

Quilt Top Diagram

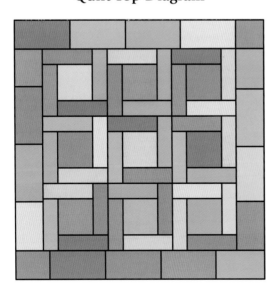

making the blocks

*Follow **Piecing** and **Pressing**, page 32, to make the Blocks. Match right sides and use ¹/₄" seam allowances throughout.*

1. Choose 1 **square** and 4 **small rectangles** for each Block.
2. Beginning at the corner and ending in the center, sew the first rectangle to the square (Fig. 1), creating a partial seam.
3. Add rectangles in a clockwise fashion to square (Fig. 2). Finish partial seam to complete Block. Make 9 Blocks.

assembling the quilt top

1. Sew 3 Blocks together to make Row. Make 3 Rows. Sew Rows together to make **Quilt Top Center.**
2. Sew 20 **large rectangles** together to create border strip.
3. Measure the Quilt Top Center from top to bottom through the center to determine length to cut **side borders**; cut 2 from border strip. Matching centers and corners, sew side borders to Quilt Top Center.
4. Measure the Quilt Top Center from side to side through the center (including added borders) to determine length to cut **top/bottom borders**; cut 2 from border strip. Matching centers and corners, sew top/bottom borders to Quilt Top Center.

completing the quilt

1. Follow **Quilting**, page 32, to mark, layer, and quilt as desired.
2. Refer to **Making a Hanging Sleeve**, page 35, to make and attach a hanging sleeve, if desired.
3. Follow **Binding**, page 36, to bind quilt using **binding strips**.

amanda

bertha

Finished Size: 24³/₄" x 27³/₄" (63 cm x 70 cm)
Finished Block Size: 3¹/₂" x 4" (9 cm x 10 cm)

fabric requirements

Yardage is based on 43"/44" (109 cm/112 cm) wide fabric.
    1 Charm Pack *or* 36 assorted 5" x 5" squares
    ¹/₄ yd (23 cm) white/light fabric for block centers
     and borders
    ¹/₄ yd (23 cm) binding fabric
    1 yd (91 cm) backing fabric
You will also need:
    33" x 36" (84 cm x 91 cm) piece of batting

cutting the pieces

*Follow **Rotary Cutting**, page 31, to cut fabric. Cut all strips from the selvage-to-selvage width of the fabric. All measurements include ¹/₄" seam allowances.*

From Charm Pack or assorted squares:
- From *each* of 36 squares, cut
  2 **short rectangles** 1¹/₂" x 2",
  2 **long rectangles** 1¹/₂" x 4¹/₂", and
  1 **border square** 2" x 2".

From white/light fabric:
- Cut 4 strips 2" wide. From these strips, cut
  36 **block centers** 2" x 2¹/₂",
  2 **short border rectangles** 2" x 9¹/₂", and
  2 **long border rectangles** 2" x 12¹/₂".

From binding fabric:
- Cut 3 **binding strips** 2¹/₄" wide.

Charm Cutting Diagram

1¹/₂" x 2"		
1¹/₂" x 2"	1¹/₂" x 4¹/₂"	1¹/₂" x 4¹/₂"
2" x 2"		

Block (make 36)

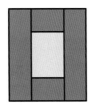

Row (make 6)

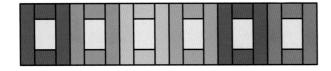

Side Border (make 2)

Top/Bottom Border (make 2)

Quilt Top Diagram

making the blocks

*Follow **Piecing** and **Pressing**, page 32, to make the Blocks. Match right sides and use ¹/₄" seam allowances throughout.*

1. Choose 1 matching set of 2 **short rectangles** and 2 **long rectangles** for each Block.

2. Sew short rectangles to top and bottom of 1 **block center**. Sew long rectangles to each side of block center to complete Block. Make 36 Blocks.

assembling the quilt top

1. Sew 6 Blocks together to make Row. Make 6 Rows. Sew Rows together to make **Quilt Top Center**.

2. Sew 4 **border squares** to each end of 1 **long border rectangle** to make side border. Make 2 side borders.

3. Sew 5 **border squares** to each end of 1 **short border rectangle** to make top/bottom border. Make 2 top/bottom borders.

4. Matching centers and corners, sew side and then top/bottom borders to Quilt Top Center.

completing the quilt

1. Follow **Quilting**, page 32, to mark, layer, and quilt as desired.

2. Refer to **Making a Hanging Sleeve**, page 35, to make and attach a hanging sleeve, if desired.

3. Follow **Binding**, page 36, to bind quilt using **binding strips**.

bertha

The quilt shown above has 36 buttons tied in the centers of the Blocks using 6 strands of cotton embroidery floss.

Note: Buttons can be a choking hazard for babies and small children.

charlotte

Finished Size: 31³/₄" x 31³/₄" (81 cm x 81 cm)
Finished Block Size: 4" x 4" (10 cm x 10 cm)

fabric requirements

Yardage is based on 43"/44" (109 cm/112 cm) wide fabric.
　　1 Charm Pack *or* 36 assorted 5" x 5" squares
　　⁷/₈ yd (80 cm) white/light fabric for blocks and
　　　borders
　　³/₈ yd (34 cm) binding fabric
　　1¹/₈ yd (1 m) backing fabric
You will also need:
　　40" x 40" (102 cm x 102 cm) piece of batting

cutting the pieces

*Follow **Rotary Cutting**, page 31, to cut fabric. Cut all strips from the selvage-to-selvage width of the fabric. All measurements include ¹/₄" seam allowances.*

From Charm Pack or assorted squares:
- From *each* of 36 squares, cut
  2 **large squares** 2¹/₂" x 2¹/₂",
  2 **small squares** 1¹/₂" x 1¹/₂", and
  1 **border rectangle** 1" x 5".

From white/light fabric:
- Cut 5 strips 2¹/₂" wide. From these strips, cut 72 **large squares** 2¹/₂" x 2¹/₂".
- Cut 2 **side inner borders** 2" x 24¹/₂".
- Cut 2 **top/bottom inner borders** 2" x 27¹/₂".
- Cut 2 **side outer borders** 2" x 28¹/₂".
- Cut 2 **top/bottom outer borders** 2" x 31¹/₂".

From binding fabric:
- Cut 4 **binding strips** 2¹/₄" wide.

Charm Cutting Diagram

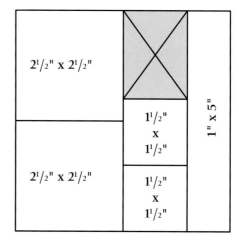

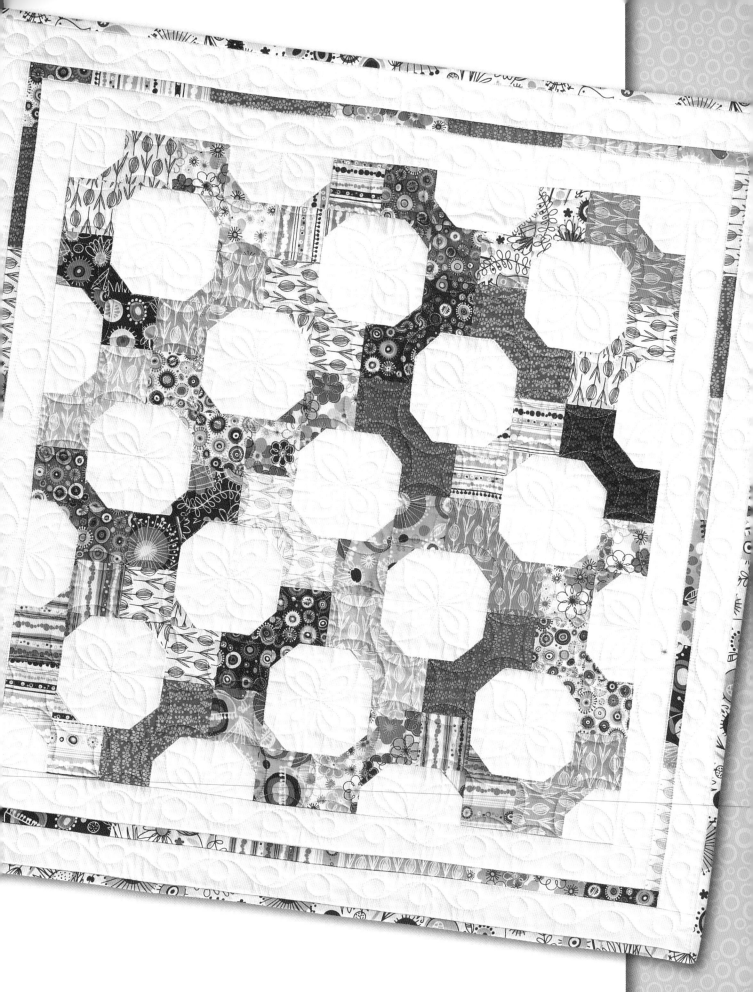

Fig. 1	Fig. 2

Stitch-and-Flip Square (make 72)

Fig. 3	Block (make 36)

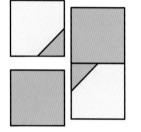 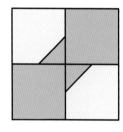

Row (make 6)

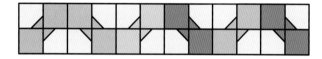

Quilt Top Diagram

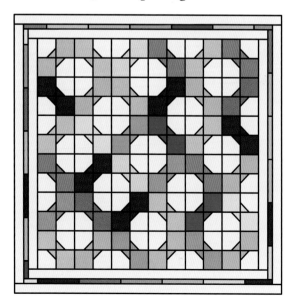

making the blocks

*Follow **Piecing** and **Pressing**, page 32, to make the Blocks. Match right sides and use ¹/₄" seam allowances throughout.*

1. Draw a diagonal line on the wrong side of each **small square**. Place 1 small square on 1 white/light **large square** and stitch diagonally as shown in Fig. 1. Trim ¹/₄" from stitching line as shown in Fig. 2; press open to complete stitch-and-flip square. Make 72 stitch-and-flip squares.
2. Sew 2 **large squares** and 2 stitch-and-flip squares of the same fabric together as shown (Fig. 3) to complete Block. Make 36 Blocks.

assembling the quilt top

1. Sew 6 Blocks together to make Row. Make 6 Rows. Alternating direction of Blocks, sew Rows together to make **Quilt Top Center.**
2. Matching centers and corners, sew **side** and then **top/bottom inner borders** to Quilt Top Center.
3. Sew 36 **border rectangles** together end to end to create border strip.
4. From this border strip, cut 2 **side pieced borders** 1" x 27¹/₂". Matching centers and corners, sew side pieced borders to Quilt Top.
5. From remainder of border strip, cut 2 **top/bottom pieced borders** 1" x 28¹/₂". Matching centers and corners, sew top/bottom pieced borders to Quilt Top.
6. Matching centers and corners, sew **side** and then **top/bottom outer borders** to Quilt Top.

completing the quilt

1. Follow **Quilting**, page 32, to mark, layer, and quilt as desired.
2. Refer to **Making a Hanging Sleeve**, page 35, to make and attach a hanging sleeve, if desired.
3. Follow **Binding**, page 36, to bind quilt using **binding strips**.

charlotte

The quilt shown above has 13 buttons tied using 6 strands of cotton embroidery floss.

Note: Buttons can be a choking hazard for babies and small children.

Finished Size: $30^{1}/_{2}$" x $30^{1}/_{2}$" (77 cm x 77 cm)
Finished Block Size: $4^{3}/_{4}$" x $4^{3}/_{4}$" (12 cm x 12 cm)

fabric requirements

Yardage is based on 43"/44" (109 cm/112 cm) wide fabric.
    1 Charm Pack *or* 25 assorted 5" x 5" squares
    $^{3}/_{8}$ yd (34 cm) white/light fabric for blocks
    $^{1}/_{2}$ yd (46 cm) fabric for border
    $^{3}/_{8}$ yd (34 cm) binding fabric
    $1^{1}/_{8}$ yds (1 m) backing fabric
You will also need:
    38" x 38" (97 cm x 97 cm) piece of batting

cutting the pieces

Follow **Rotary Cutting**, *page 31, to cut fabric. Cut all strips from the selvage-to-selvage width of the fabric. All measurements include $^{1}/_{4}$" seam allowances.*

From Charm Pack or assorted squares:
  • From *each* of 25 squares, cut 2 **rectangles A** $2^{1}/_{2}$" x 5".
From white/light fabric:
  • Cut 7 strips $1^{1}/_{4}$" wide. From these strips, cut 25 **rectangles B** $1^{1}/_{4}$" x 5", and 25 **rectangles C** $1^{1}/_{4}$" x $5^{1}/_{4}$".
From border fabric:
  • Cut 2 **side borders** $3^{1}/_{2}$" x $24^{1}/_{4}$".
  • Cut 2 **top/bottom borders** $3^{1}/_{2}$" x $30^{1}/_{4}$".
From binding fabric:
  • Cut 4 **binding strips** $2^{1}/_{4}$" wide.

Charm Cutting Diagram

$2^{1}/_{2}$" x 5"
$2^{1}/_{2}$" x 5"

Fig. 1   **Unit 1** (make 25)

Fig. 2   **Block** (make 25)

Row (make 5)

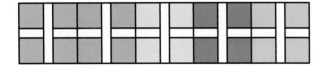

Quilt Top Diagram

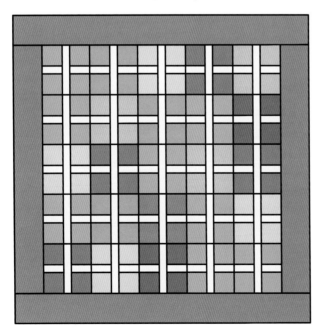

making the blocks

*Follow **Piecing** and **Pressing**, page 32, to make the Blocks. Match right sides and use ¹/₄" seam allowances throughout.*

1. Sew 2 matching **rectangles A** to 1 **rectangle B** (Fig. 1) to make Unit 1. Make 25 Unit 1's.
2. Cut Unit 1 in half (Fig. 2). Sew 1 half to each side of 1 **rectangle C** to complete Block. Make 25 Blocks.

assembling the quilt top

1. Sew 5 Blocks together to make Row. Make 5 Rows. Sew Rows together to make **Quilt Top Center.**
2. Matching centers and corners, sew **side** and then **top/bottom borders** to Quilt Top Center.

completing the quilt

1. Follow **Quilting**, page 32, to mark, layer, and quilt as desired.
2. Refer to **Making a Hanging Sleeve**, page 35, to make and attach a hanging sleeve, if desired.
3. Follow **Binding**, page 36, to bind quilt using **binding strips.**

dora

These slightly smaller Dora quilts have narrower borders. To make one of these quilts, cut 2 **side borders** $2^3/_4$" x $24^1/_4$" and 2 **top/bottom borders** $2^3/_4$" x $28^3/_4$". The finished size of each quilt is 29" x 29" (74 cm x 74 cm).

Finished Size: 34¹/₄" x 37¹/₄" (87 cm x 95 cm)

fabric requirements

Yardage is based on 43"/44" (109 cm/112 cm) wide fabric.

    1 Charm Pack *or* 30 assorted 5" x 5" squares
    ⁷/₈ yd (80 cm) fabric for sashings and border
    ³/₈ yd (34 cm) binding fabric
    2¹/₂ yds (2.3 m) backing fabric
You will also need:
    42" x 45" (107 cm x 114 cm) piece of batting

cutting the pieces

*Follow **Rotary Cutting**, page 31, to cut fabric. Cut all strips from the selvage-to-selvage width of the fabric. All measurements include ¹/₄" seam allowances.*

From Charm Pack or assorted squares:
- From *each* of 30 squares, cut 2 **rectangles** 2¹/₂" x 5".

From fabric for sashings and border:
- Cut 3 **sashing strips** 3¹/₂" x 30¹/₂".
- Cut 2 **side borders** 3³/₄" x 30¹/₂".
- Cut 2 **top/bottom borders** 3³/₄" x 34".

From binding fabric:
- Cut 4 **binding strips** 2¹/₄" wide.

Charm Cutting Diagram

2¹/₂" x 5"
2¹/₂" x 5"

Row (make 4)

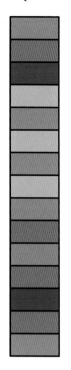

Quilt Top Center

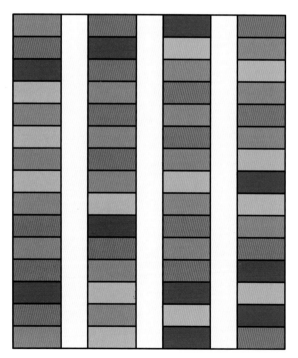

assembling the quilt top

*Follow **Piecing** and **Pressing**, page 32, to make the Rows. Match right sides and use ¹/₄" seam allowances throughout.*

1. Sew 15 **rectangles** together to make vertical Row. Make 4 Rows.
2. Sew **sashing strips** and **Rows** together to complete Quilt Top Center.
3. Matching centers and corners, sew **side** and then **top/bottom borders** to Quilt Top Center.

completing the quilt

1. Follow **Quilting**, page 32, to mark, layer, and quilt as desired.
2. Refer to **Making a Hanging Sleeve**, page 35, to make and attach a hanging sleeve, if desired.
3. Follow **Binding**, page 36, to bind quilt using **binding strips**.

Tip: To make this charming quilt larger, simply add a second border!

emma

The quilt shown above has the sashings and border cut *lengthwise* from stripe fabric. For this, you will need $1^1/_8$ yds (1 m) of fabric.

Finished Size: 38³/₄" x 42³/₄" (98 cm x 109 cm)
Finished Block Size: 6" x 6" (15 cm x 15 cm)

fabric requirements

Yardage is based on 43"/44" (109 cm/112 cm) wide fabric.
    1 Charm Pack *or* 42 assorted 5" x 5" squares
    ¹/₂ yd (46 cm) white/light fabric for blocks
    ³/₈ yd (34 cm) fabric for inner border
    ¹/₄ yd (23 cm) fabric for middle border
    ³/₈ yd (34 cm) fabric for outer border
    ³/₈ yd (34 cm) binding fabric
    2⁷/₈ yds (2.6 m) backing fabric
You will also need:
    47" x 51" (119 cm x 130 cm) piece of batting

cutting the pieces

*Follow **Rotary Cutting**, page 31, to cut fabric. Cut all strips from the selvage-to-selvage width of the fabric. All measurements include ¹/₄" seam allowances.*

From Charm Pack or assorted squares:
- Select 12 squares for block centers. From each of these, cut 1 **large square** 4" x 4" (**cutting diagram A**).
- Select 30 squares for Nine Patch Blocks. From each of these, cut 4 **small squares** 2¹/₂" x 2¹/₂" (**cutting diagram B**).

From white/light fabric:
- Cut 3 strips 5" wide. From these, cut 24 squares 5" x 5". Cut these *once* diagonally to make 48 **triangles**.

From fabric for inner border:
- Cut 2 **side inner borders** 2¹/₂" x 30¹/₂".
- Cut 2 **top/bottom inner borders** 2¹/₂" x 34¹/₂".

From fabric for middle border:
- Cut 2 **top/bottom middle borders** 2¹/₂" x 34¹/₂".

From fabric for outer border:
- Cut 2 **side outer borders** 2¹/₂" x 38¹/₂".
- Cut 2 **top/bottom outer borders** 2¹/₂" x 38¹/₂".

From binding fabric:
- Cut 5 **binding strips** 2¹/₄" wide.

Charm Cutting Diagram A

4" x 4"

Charm Cutting Diagram B

2¹/₂" x 2¹/₂"	2¹/₂" x 2¹/₂"
2¹/₂" x 2¹/₂"	2¹/₂" x 2¹/₂"

Unit 1
(make 39)

Nine Patch Block
(make 13)

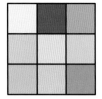

Fig. 1

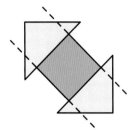

Square-in-a-Square Block (make 12)

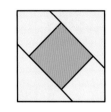

Row A (make 3)

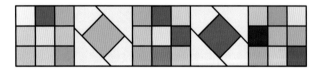

Row B (make 2)

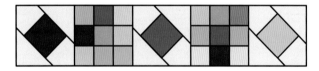

Quilt Top Center

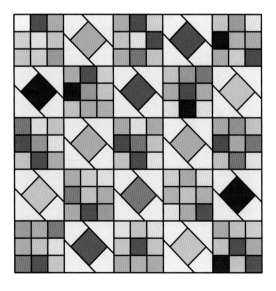

making the blocks

*Follow **Piecing** and **Pressing**, page 32, to make the Blocks. Match right sides and use ¹/₄" seam allowances throughout.*

1. Sew 3 **small squares** together to make **Unit 1**. Make 39 Unit 1's.
2. Sew 3 Unit 1's together to complete **Nine Patch Block**. Make 13 Nine Patch Blocks.
3. Fold and crease to mark the centers of long edges of 4 **triangles** and all edges of 1 **large square**. Matching center marks, sew 2 triangles to large square as shown; trim triangles even with large square (**Fig. 1**).
4. Matching center marks, sew 2 triangles to remaining sides of large square. Trim to 6¹/₂" x 6¹/₂" to complete **Square-in-a-Square Block**. Make 12 Square-in-a-Square Blocks.

assembling the quilt top

1. Sew 3 Nine Patch Blocks and 2 Square-in-a-Square Blocks together to complete **Row A**. Make 3 Row A's.
2. Sew 2 Nine Patch Blocks and 3 Square-in-a-Square Blocks together to complete **Row B**. Make 2 Row B's.
3. Sew Row A's and B's together to complete **Quilt Top Center**.
4. Matching centers and corners, sew **side** and then **top/bottom inner borders** to Quilt Top Center.
5. Matching centers and corners, sew **top/bottom middle borders** to Quilt Top.
6. Matching centers and corners, sew **side** and then **top/bottom outer borders** to Quilt Top.

completing the quilt

1. Follow **Quilting**, page 32, to mark, layer, and quilt as desired.
2. Refer to **Making a Hanging Sleeve**, page 35, to make and attach a hanging sleeve, if desired.
3. Follow **Binding**, page 36, to bind quilt using **binding strips**.

fiona

25

Finished Size: 36¹/₄" x 36¹/₄" (92 cm x 92 cm)
Finished Block Size: 8" x 8" (20 cm x 20 cm)

fabric requirements

Yardage is based on 43"/44" (109 cm/112 cm) wide fabric.

 1 Charm Pack *or* 36 assorted 5" x 5" squares
 ¹/₂ yd (46 cm) fabric for sashings and inner border
 ¹/₂ yd (46 cm) fabric for outer border
 ³/₈ yd (34 cm) binding fabric
 2¹/₂ yds (2.3 m) backing fabric

You will also need:

 44" x 44" (112 cm x 112 cm) piece of batting

cutting the pieces

*Follow **Rotary Cutting**, page 31, to cut fabric. Cut all strips from the selvage-to-selvage width of the fabric. All measurements include ¹/₄" seam allowances.*

From Charm Pack or assorted squares:
- From each square, cut
  1 **square** 3¹/₂" x 3¹/₂" ,
  1 **short rectangle** 1¹/₂" x 3¹/₂", and
  1 **long rectangle** 1¹/₂" x 4¹/₂".

From fabric for sashings and inner border:
- Cut 2 strips 2" wide. From these, cut
  6 **sashing rectangles** 2" x 8¹/₂".
- Cut 2 **sashing strips** 2" x 27¹/₂".
- Cut 2 **side inner borders** 2" x 27¹/₂".
- Cut 2 **top/bottom inner borders** 2" x 30¹/₂".

From fabric for outer border:
- Cut 2 **side outer borders** 3¹/₄" x 30¹/₂".
- Cut 2 **top/bottom outer borders** 3¹/₄" x 36".

From binding fabric:
- Cut 4 **binding strips** 2¹/₄" wide.

Charm Cutting Diagram

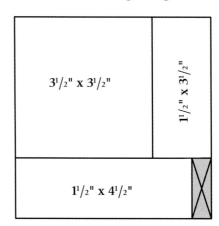

3¹/₂" x 3¹/₂"

1¹/₂" x 3¹/₂"

1¹/₂" x 4¹/₂"

Unit 1 (make 36)

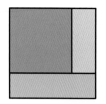

Block (make 9)

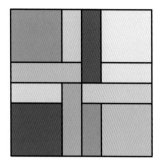

Row (make 3)

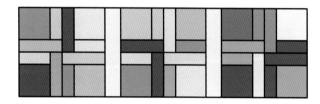

Quilt Top Center

making the blocks

*Follow **Piecing** and **Pressing**, page 32, to make the Blocks. Match right sides and use ¹/₄" seam allowances throughout.*

1. Sew 1 **square**, 1 **short rectangle** and 1 **long rectangle** together to make Unit 1. Make 36 Unit 1's.
2. Sew 4 Unit 1's together to complete Block. Make 9 Blocks.

assembling the quilt top

1. Sew 3 Blocks and 2 **sashing rectangles** together to complete Row. Make 3 Rows.
2. Sew 3 Rows and 2 **sashing strips** together complete Quilt Top Center.
3. Matching centers and corners, sew **side** and then **top/bottom inner borders** to Quilt Top Center.
4. Matching centers and corners, sew **side** and then **top/bottom outer borders** to Quilt Top.

completing the quilt

1. Follow **Quilting**, page 32, to mark, layer, and quilt as desired.
2. Refer to **Making a Hanging Sleeve**, page 35, to make and attach a hanging sleeve, if desired.
3. Follow **Binding**, page 36, to bind quilt using **binding strips**.

greta

29

To make your quilting easier and more enjoyable, we encourage you to carefully read all of the general instructions, study the color photographs, and familiarize yourself with the individual project instructions before beginning a project.

fabrics

selecting fabrics

Choose high-quality, medium-weight 100% cotton fabrics. All-cotton fabrics hold a crease better, fray less, and are easier to quilt than cotton/polyester blends.

Yardage requirements listed for each project are based on 43"/44" wide fabric with a "usable" width of 40" after shrinkage and trimming selvages. Actual usable width will probably vary slightly from fabric to fabric. Our recommended yardage lengths should be adequate for occasional re-squaring of fabric when many cuts are required.

These designs are perfect for pre-cut charm packs, collections of 5" x 5" squares. Each project lists the number of squares you will need. Always check the number of pieces in a charm pack against your pattern requirements.

preparing fabrics

We do not recommend pre-washing your yardage or charm squares. Pre-washing fabrics may distort the fabric and may cause the edges to ravel. As a result, your charm squares may not be large enough to cut all of the pieces required for your chosen project. Refer to **Caring for Your Quilt**, page 39, for instructions on washing your finished quilt.

We do recommend that you prepare fabrics before cutting with a steam iron set on cotton and starch or sizing. The starch or sizing will give the fabric a crisp finish. This will make cutting more accurate and may make piecing easier.

rotary cutting

Rotary cutting has brought speed and accuracy to quiltmaking by allowing quilters to easily cut strips of fabric and then cut those strips into smaller pieces.

- Place fabric on work surface with fold closest to you.

- Cut all strips from the selvage-to-selvage width of the fabric unless otherwise indicated in project instructions.

- Square left edge of fabric using rotary cutter and rulers (Figs. 1 – 2).

Fig. 1

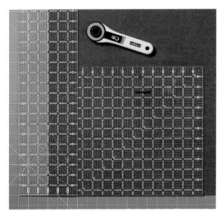

Fig. 2

- To cut each strip required for a project, place ruler over cut edge of fabric, aligning desired marking on ruler with cut edge; make cut (Fig. 3).

Fig. 3

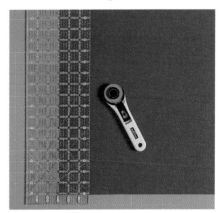

- When cutting several strips from a single piece of fabric, it is important to make sure that cuts remain at a perfect right angle to the fold; square fabric as needed.

- Many charm squares have pinked edges and most manufacturers include the points of the pinked edges in the measurement given on the package. Before cutting squares into smaller pieces, measure your squares to determine if you need to include the points to achieve the correct cut size.

piecing

Precise cutting, followed by accurate piecing, will ensure that all pieces of quilt top fit together well.

- Set sewing machine stitch length for approximately 11 stitches per inch.

- Use neutral-colored general-purpose sewing thread (not quilting thread) in needle and in bobbin.

- An accurate $^1/_4$" seam allowance is *essential*. Presser feet that are $^1/_4$" wide are available for most sewing machines.

- When piecing, always place pieces right sides together and match raw edges; pin if necessary.

- Chain piecing saves time and will usually result in more accurate piecing.

- For an accurate seam allowance when piecing charm squares with pinked edges, measure from point to point across the center of the square. If it measures exactly 5" x 5", align the tip of the points with your $^1/_4$" seam guide when sewing. If it is larger or smaller, take a larger or smaller seam allowance accordingly.

sewing across seam intersections

When sewing across intersection of two seams, place pieces right sides together and match seams exactly, making sure seam allowances are pressed in opposite directions (Fig. 4).

Fig. 4

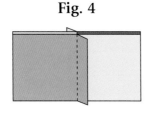

pressing

- Use steam iron set on "Cotton" for all pressing.

- Press after sewing each seam.

- Seam allowances are almost always pressed to one side, usually toward darker fabric. However, to reduce bulk it may occasionally be necessary to press seam allowances toward the lighter fabric or even to press them open.

- To prevent dark fabric seam allowance from showing through light fabric, trim darker seam allowance slightly narrower than lighter seam allowance.

quilting

*Quilting holds the three layers (top, batting, and backing) of the quilt together and can be done by hand or machine. Because marking, layering, and quilting are interrelated and may be done in different orders depending on circumstances, please read entire **Quilting** section, pages 32–35, before beginning project.*

marking quilting lines

Quilting lines may be marked using fabric marking pencils, chalk markers, or water- or air-soluble pens.

Simple quilting designs may be marked with chalk or chalk pencil after basting. A small area may be marked, then quilted, before moving to next area to be marked. Intricate designs should be marked before basting using a more durable marker.

Caution: Pressing may permanently set some marks. **Test** different markers **on scrap fabric** to find one that marks clearly and can be thoroughly removed.

A wide variety of pre-cut quilting stencils, as well as entire books of quilting patterns, are available. Using a stencil makes it easier to mark intricate or repetitive designs.

To make a stencil from a pattern, center template plastic over pattern and use a permanent marker to trace pattern onto plastic. Use a craft knife with single or double blade to cut channels along traced lines (Fig. 5).

Fig. 5

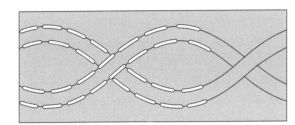

preparing the backing
To allow for slight shifting of quilt top during quilting, backing should be approximately 4" larger on all sides. Yardage requirements listed for quilt backings are calculated for 43"/44"w fabric. To piece a backing using 43"/44"w fabric, use the following instructions.

1. Measure length and width of quilt top; add 8" to each measurement.

2. Cut backing fabric into two lengths slightly longer than determined *length* measurement. Trim selvages. Place lengths with right sides facing and sew long edges together, forming tube (Fig. 6). Match seams and press along one fold (Fig. 7). Cut along pressed fold to form single piece (Fig. 8).

Fig. 6	**Fig. 7**

Fig. 8

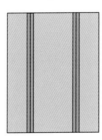

3. Trim backing to size determined in Step 1; press seam allowances open.

choosing the batting

The appropriate batting will make quilting easier. For fine hand quilting, choose low-loft batting. All cotton or cotton/polyester blend battings work well for machine quilting because the cotton helps "grip" quilt layers. If quilt is to be tied, a high-loft batting, sometimes called extra-loft or fat batting, may be used to make quilt "fluffy."

Types of batting include cotton, polyester, wool, cotton/polyester blend, cotton/wool blend, and silk.

When selecting batting, refer to package labels for characteristics and care instructions. Cut batting same size as prepared backing.

assembling the quilt

1. Examine wrong side of quilt top closely; trim any seam allowances and clip any threads that may show through front of the quilt. Press quilt top, being careful not to "set" any marked quilting lines.

2. Place backing *wrong* side up on flat surface. Use masking tape to tape edges of backing to surface. Place batting on top of backing fabric. Smooth batting gently, being careful not to stretch or tear. Center quilt top *right* side up on batting.

3. If machine quilting, use 1" rustproof safety pins to "pin-baste" all layers together, spacing pins approximately 4" apart. Begin at center and work toward outer edges to secure all layers. If possible, place pins away from areas that will be quilted, although pins may be removed as needed when quilting.

machine quilting methods

Use general-purpose thread in bobbin. Do not use quilting thread. Thread the needle of machine with general-purpose thread or transparent monofilament thread to make quilting blend with quilt top fabrics. Use decorative thread, such as a metallic or contrasting-color general-purpose thread, to make quilting lines stand out more.

Straight-Line Quilting

The term "straight-line" is somewhat deceptive, since curves (especially gentle ones) as well as straight lines can be stitched with this technique.

1. Set stitch length for six to ten stitches per inch and attach walking foot to sewing machine.

2. Determine which section of quilt will have longest continuous quilting line, oftentimes area from center top to center bottom. Roll up and secure each edge of quilt to help reduce the bulk, keeping fabrics smooth. Smaller projects may not need to be rolled.

3. Begin stitching on longest quilting line, using very short stitches for the first $^1/_4$" to "lock" quilting. Stitch across project, using one hand on each side of walking foot to slightly spread fabric and to guide fabric through machine. Lock stitches at end of quilting line.

4. Continue machine quilting, stitching longer quilting lines first to stabilize quilt before moving on to other areas.

Free-Motion Quilting

Free-motion quilting may be free form or may follow a marked pattern.

1. Attach darning foot to sewing machine and lower or cover feed dogs.

2. Position quilt under darning foot; lower foot. Holding top thread, take a stitch and pull bobbin thread to top of quilt. To "lock" beginning of quilting line, hold top and bobbin threads while making three to five stitches in place.

3. Use one hand on each side of darning foot to slightly spread fabric and to move fabric through the machine. Even stitch length is achieved by using smooth, flowing hand motion and steady machine speed. Slow machine speed and fast hand movement will create long stitches. Fast machine speed and slow hand movement will create short stitches. Move quilt sideways, back and forth, in a circular motion, or in a random motion to create desired designs; do not rotate quilt. Lock stitches at end of each quilting line.

making a hanging sleeve

Attaching a hanging sleeve to the back of a quilt before the binding is added allows the quilt to be displayed on a wall.

1. Measure width of quilt top edge and subtract 1". Cut piece of fabric 7"w by determined measurement.

2. Press short edges of fabric piece $1/4$" to wrong side; press edges $1/4$" to wrong side again and machine stitch in place.

3. Matching wrong sides, fold piece in half lengthwise to form tube.

4. Follow project instructions to sew binding to quilt top and to trim backing and batting. Before Blindstitching binding to backing, match raw edges and stitch hanging sleeve to center top edge on back of quilt.

5. Finish binding quilt, treating hanging sleeve as part of backing.

6. Blindstitch bottom of hanging sleeve to backing, taking care not to stitch through to front of quilt.

7. Insert dowel or slat into hanging sleeve.

binding
Binding encloses the raw edges of quilt.

1. Using a diagonal seam (Fig. 9), sew binding strips called for in project together end to end.

Fig. 9

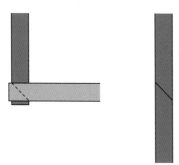

2. Matching wrong sides and long edges, press strip in half to make binding.

3. Beginning with one end near center on bottom edge of quilt, lay binding around quilt to make sure that seams in binding will not end up at a corner. Adjust placement if necessary. Matching raw edges of binding to raw edge of quilt top, pin binding to right side of quilt along one edge.

4. When you reach first corner, mark ¹/₄" from corner of quilt top (Fig. 10).

Fig. 10

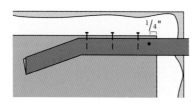

5. Beginning approximately 10" from end of binding and using ¹/₄" seam allowance, sew binding to quilt, backstitching at beginning of stitching and at mark (Fig. 11). Lift needle out of fabric and clip thread.

Fig. 11

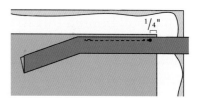

6. Fold binding as shown in Figs. 12–13 and pin binding to adjacent side, matching raw edges. When you've reached the next corner, mark ¹/₄" from edge of quilt top.

Fig. 12

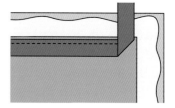

Fig. 13

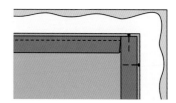

7. Backstitching at edge of quilt top, sew pinned binding to quilt (Fig. 14); backstitch at the next mark. Lift needle out of fabric and clip thread.

Fig. 14

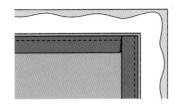

8. Continue sewing binding to quilt, stopping approximately 10" from starting point (Fig. 15).

Fig. 15

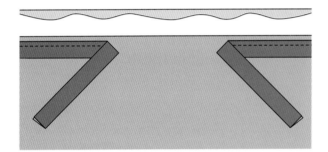

9. Bring beginning and end of binding to center of opening and fold each end back, leaving a $1/4$" space between folds (Fig. 16). Finger press folds.

Fig. 16

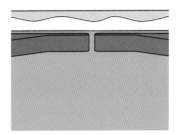

10. Unfold ends of binding and draw a line across wrong side in finger-pressed crease. Draw a line through the lengthwise pressed fold of binding at the same spot to create a cross mark. With edge of ruler at cross mark, line up 45° angle marking on ruler with one long side of binding. Draw a diagonal line from edge to edge. Repeat on remaining end, making sure that the two diagonal lines are angled the same way (Fig. 17).

Fig. 17

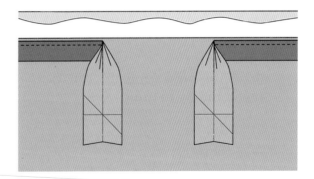

11. Matching right sides and diagonal lines, pin binding ends together at right angles (Fig. 18).

Fig. 18

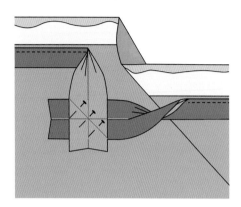

12. Machine stitch along diagonal line (Fig. 19), removing pins as you stitch.

Fig. 19

13. Lay binding against quilt to double check that it is correct length.

14. Trim binding ends, leaving ¼" seam allowance; press seam allowances open. Stitch binding to quilt.

15. Trim backing and batting even with edges of quilt top.

16. On one edge of quilt, fold binding over to quilt backing and pin pressed edge in place, covering stitching line (Fig 20). On adjacent side, fold binding over, forming a mitered corner (Fig. 21). Repeat to pin remainder of binding in place.

Fig. 20   **Fig. 21**

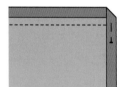 

17. Blindstitch binding to backing, taking care not to stitch through to front of quilt. To Blindstitch, come up at 1, go down at 2, and come up at 3 (Fig. 22).

Fig. 22

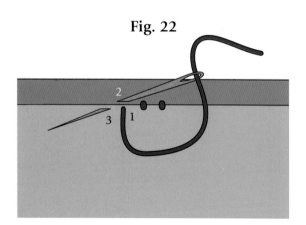

signing and dating your quilt

A completed quilt is a work of art and should be signed and dated. There are many different ways to do this and numerous books on the subject. The label should reflect the style of the quilt, the occasion or person for which it was made, and the quilter's own particular talents. Following are suggestions for recording the history of quilt or adding a sentiment for future generations.

- Embroider quilter's name, date, and any additional information on quilt top or backing. Matching floss, such as cream floss on white/light border, will leave a subtle record. Bright or contrasting floss will make the information stand out.

- Make label from muslin and use permanent marker to write information. Use different colored permanent markers to make label more decorative. Stitch label to back of quilt.

- Use photo-transfer paper to add image to white or cream fabric label. Stitch label to back of quilt.

- Piece an extra block from quilt top pattern to use as label. Add information with permanent fabric pen. Appliqué block to back of quilt.

caring for your quilt

- Wash finished quilt in cold water on gentle cycle with mild soap. Soaps which have no softeners, fragrances, whiteners, or other additives are safest. Rinse twice in cold water.

- Use a dye magnet, such as Shout® Color Catcher®, each time quilt is washed to absorb any dyes that bleed.

- Dry quilt on low heat/air fluff in 15 minute increments until dry.

Metric Conversion Chart

Inches x 2.54 = centimeters (cm)
Inches x 25.4 = millimeters (mm)
Inches x .0254 = meters (m)

Yards x .9144 = meters (m)
Yards x 91.44 = centimeters (cm)
Centimeters x .3937 = inches (")
Meters x 1.0936 = yards (yd)

Standard Equivalents

1/8"	3.2 mm	0.32 cm	1/8 yard	11.43 cm	0.11 m
1/4"	6.35 mm	0.635 cm	1/4 yard	22.86 cm	0.23 m
3/8"	9.5 mm	0.95 cm	3/8 yard	34.29 cm	0.34 m
1/2"	12.7 mm	1.27 cm	1/2 yard	45.72 cm	0.46 m
5/8"	15.9 mm	1.59 cm	5/8 yard	57.15 cm	0.57 m
3/4"	19.1 mm	1.91 cm	3/4 yard	68.58 cm	0.69 m
7/8"	22.2 mm	2.22 cm	7/8 yard	80 cm	0.8 m
1"	25.4 mm	2.54 cm	1 yard	91.44 cm	0.91 m

production team

Technical Editor – Lisa Lancaster
Technical Writer – Frances Huddleston
Editorial Writer – Susan McManus Johnson
Senior Graphic Artist – Lora Puls
Graphic Artists – Amy Temple, Jacob Casleton, Becca Snider, and Janie Marie Wright
Photographer – Ken West

We have made every effort to ensure that these instructions are accurate and complete. We cannot, however, be responsible for human error, typographical mistakes, or variations in individual work.